Kurious Kids Book about Lying I, Lying II and Sharing

Brian Smith

Kurious Kids Book aboutLying I ,Lying II and Sharing Label
©2015, Brian Smith All rights reserved.

This eBook and supplementary material was created to provide specific information regarding the subject matter covered. Every attempt has been made to verify the information provided in this material however neither the author nor the publisher are responsible for any errors, omissions, or incorrect interpretations of the subject matter.

Information contained within this material is subject to local, state, federal and international laws. The reader is advised to consult with a licensed professional for legal, financial and other professional services.

The reader of this material assumes responsibility for the use of this information. Adherence to all applicable laws and regulations governing professional licensing, business practices, advertising and all other aspects of doing business in the United States or any other jurisdiction is the sole responsibility of the reader.

The author and publisher assume no responsibility or liability whatsoever for the use or misuse of the information contained within these materials.

All rights reserved. No part of this publication may be reproduced, distributed, or transmitted in any form or by any means, including photocopying, recording, or other electronic or mechanical methods, without the prior written permission of the publisher, except in the case of brief quotations embodied in critical reviews and certain other noncommercial uses permitted by copyright law.

From the Desk James Moore Editor of Bull City Publishing:

Dear Friend,

If at Any point while you're reading this book you have any questions, please don't hesitate to contact us. You can best reach us at Twitter (@bullcitypub), or on our Facebook Fan Page

Even if you don't have any questions, We'd love for you to come by and say hello! If you want to reach us in a private you can email us at info@bullcitypublishing.com or on our blog Bullcitypublishing.com/blog

Warmest Regards,

James Moore

Editor & Chief ,Bull City Publishing, LLC

Do you Love Reading? Do you Want a Ton of FREE Kindle Books? Join our Mailing list by Emailing us at freebooks@bullcitypublishing.com

Disclaimer

The subject matter contained within is an original work. It is intended for 'informational and educational' purposes and the reader is encouraged to practice all diligence prior to the application of any subject matter in copy herein.

The Kurious Kid Presents™:

Lying & Tell The Truth

Part 1

The Kurious Kd Presents™:

Lying Part II

The Kurious Kid Presents™:

Sharing

Table of Contents

The Kurious Kid Presents™: Lying & Tell The Truth Part 1 1

ALL ABOUT LYING 2

Introduction 3

Conclusion 24

The Kurious Kid Presents™: Lying Part II 26

Introduction 27

The Kurious Kid Presents™: Sharing 42

Think About Sharing 43

The Kurious Kid Presents™:
Lying & Tell The Truth
Part 1

ALL ABOUT LYING

Summary

A lie is a false statement that is made to represent the truth. It is often said to deceive or trick someone. Anyone can tell a lie. Even animals do it. Telling lies affect not only you but all those around you. We sometimes lie to protect ourselves or someone else however, it is always better to tell the truth.

It is possible to detect when people are lying through technology. Lying has consequences which get more serious as we get older. Telling lies makes people distrust you and robs you of enjoying many things. There is never a good enough reason to lie.

INTRODUCTION

You might have heard your parents tell you to never tell lies and wondered why? You may have also wondered: what exactly are lies and why is it so terrible to tell one? It is always good to have questions because questions encourage you to learn, when you find the answers to them.

All About Lying will provide you with the answers that you are looking for and hopefully steer you in the right direction towards becoming an *honest* person. You will understand what lies are, who tells them, and how they affect you and those around you. You will also learn of the consequences that follow lying and the rewards that follow the truth. Ultimately, it will be up to you to decide whether you want to be an honest person or a Liar.

What is a lie?

A lie is a false statement that is made to represent the truth. It is often said to deceive or trick someone. What this means is that instead of saying what actually happened when asked about something you did or witnessed, you tell a made up version.

A lie is not the same as playing make-believe or pretending.

It's okay to pretend, but not okay to lie.

Sometimes we may dress up as a princess or a cowboy and prance around the house slaying dragons and riding horses. That is okay, as long as it remains a game.

When we play games, accidents can and do happen.

Accidents can happen.

We may accidentally knock over a vase, empty a closet and even get our Sunday clothes dirty, when we play games. We are all a little clumsy at times. This is all part of having fun and no one is punished for accidents. When however, we lie about those accidents, we can get into serious trouble.

Who lies?

A person who tells a lie is often called a 'Liar'.

If you don't like being called a Liar, don't tell lies.

Telling a single lie can affect what people think of you. When we tell the truth, we earn the, trust, love and respect of others. When we tell lies, we make people distrust us and therefore not like us.

Kurious Kids Book about
Lying I ,Lying II and Sharing

Lying can make people dislike you.

But who tells lies anyway?

Anyone and everyone can tell a lie. The young, old, any gender and any race, can tell lies. Even animals lie!

Even animals try to get away with being naughty.

How do animals lie? You may be wondering since they do not speak like you do. To understand how animals can lie, you must be aware that Lying is done through the use of words or verbally and through facial and body gestures, or non-verbally. Scientists know that animals have other ways of communicating to each other such as through sounds and actions. They are as much capable of lying as we are.

How do we lie?

You may wonder, how do we lie or rather how would someone know that we are lying? There is no shame in wondering, but there is shame is lying.

A mess is less messy than a lie.

Lying verbally may be as simple as saying "no" when we are asked if we did something and the truth would be "yes". Can you remember a time when you did something that was wrong and when you were asked if you did it, you said "no"? Do you also remember how you felt when you lied? Sometimes when we tell a lie we can feel very anxious. We may be hot or our heart begins to beat faster. Some of us even sweat or fidget. Overall when we lie, we do not feel good.

Lying non-verbally may also be as simple as shrugging our shoulders as if to say "I don't know", when the truth is that we know exactly what happened. In this case we may be trying to protect a friend or ourselves.

Because when we lie our bodies also give off physical cues such as stuttering, sweating, fidgeting and fast breathing, even when we think that no one knows if we are lying or not, someone who is trained to detect the physical signs of lying can determine the truth.

Your face may be telling a different story.

People who work in law enforcement are usually trained to detect the verbal and non-verbal cues that reveal whether or not someone is being truthful. Technology has also allowed people to detect signs that cannot be seen with the naked eye, such as your heart beat. You may have heard the term "Lie Detector", before and wondered if it is an actual person.

A lie detector is in fact a machine that is attached to the person suspected of lying. It records the heartbeat of the person and can alert the operator of any changes which would suggest an attempt to deceive or trick.

In the story of Pinocchio, his nose grew every time he told a lie. Pinocchio had many faults and deliberately lied when he had the opportunity to tell the truth. Our noses may not grow when we try to deceive or trick others but there are other signs that may give us away. The truth can be written all over our faces and we just don't know it. Even as we tell a lie and feel assured that no one knows the truth, our bodies may be giving off signs that say otherwise. At the end of the story, Pinocchio learned about the consequences of lying, but we do not have to wait until we are punished to learn that lying is wrong.

Why do we lie?

If we know that lying makes people distrust us and also gets us in trouble then why do people lie anyways?

Lies are often told to hide the truth because the person who lies is afraid of being punished, does not want to hurt someone else's feelings or simply want to get something. If we are trying to protect someone's feelings, we may feel that lying is necessary. If we did something that was bad and do not want to be punished, then fear may make us want to lie. Also if we know that we want something really badly and are not will to do what is necessary to get it, then we may find it easier to lie just to get it.

Kurious Kids Book about
Lying I ,Lying II and Sharing

A belly full of truth is better than a mouthful of lies.

Not all lies are told because of fear, pride or greed though. Sometimes people lie for the fun of it. Take for example when playing a game, sometimes one player tells lies so that they can gain some advantage over the other. This is also called 'Cheating'. Even though it may be in fun, it is important to remember that a lie is a lie.

Lies can be very destructive. It is always better to tell the truth even when you are afraid that you may be punished. If you lie to win a game then you may not be able to celebrate your victory because it was not achieved fairly. In the Olympics for example, if you lie or cheat to win a game, you can have your medals taken away and be barred from ever competing again. Imagine if your favorite athlete and hero turned out to be a dishonest person. You would not only be disappointed and hurt but you will have less respect for than person because they did not earn your respect and adoration through honesty.

Telling the truth is not as scary as you think!

Sometimes people lie so that they can get people to do what they want. Consider the moral of the story, 'The Boy Who Cried Wolf'. He kept lying about the wolf coming for his sheep so that he could get attention from the towns people, but when the people of the town realized that there was no wolf and the boy was simply lying for the fun of it, they stopped running out to help him save the sheep. In the end, the wolf really came and when the boy cried for help, no one believed that he was in trouble. The wolf then gobbled up all the sheep.

Although in the real world there may not be any wolf lurking about to eat your sheep, when you lie about something to get people to react, it can back fire. Once people become aware that you are telling a lie, it is very difficult for them to believe you when you are indeed telling the truth.

Kurious Kids Book about
Lying I ,Lying II and Sharing

Only a liar can't stand to wear his own clothes.

Lying to get what you want is also very bad. Consider the toy that you want for Christmas. Your parents may have promised you that if you did your homework on time, you would be rewarded with that toy.

You may want to trick them because you find doing your homework takes up too much time.

Trying is better than Lying.

If you lie about not having homework, it can mean bad news for you. Your teacher may write a report that will eventually be given to your parents and this will make them very upset. Also not doing your homework can rob you of the learning rewards. You may find it hard to follow along in class and even harder to answer questions when you are called upon. All in all a lie makes life difficult for everyone.

Kurious Kids Book about
Lying I ,Lying II and Sharing

When you tell lies they soon stack up against you.

Lying to avoid being punished can have many negative consequences. If you made a mistake for example, such as throwing a ball through a neighbor's window, breaking it, it is important to tell the truth. Blaming it on someone else can result in another person being punished for what you did. If you lie about what you did, your neighbor may become very angry with your parents and they can be punished for what you did. Consider telling the truth. If you tell the truth there is a very strong possibility that your neighbor will respect you for being honest. You may still have to help fix the window or offer some other type of compensation, but at least you will not be labeled a Liar.

Lies catch up to you, no matter how fast you run from them.

Whether our intentions are good or not, Lying is always wrong. Lying can also be very embarrassing. Take for example a situation where you saw something and decided to lie about seeing it. Someone else might have been looking at you when this happened and they may be brave enough to tell the truth. As a result, you may wind up being labeled a Liar.

Kurious Kids Book about
Lying I ,Lying II and Sharing

What's uglier than a bully? A lie!

What are the Consequences of Lying?

If you have never told a lie before then you may not have experienced the consequences of lying. When we are young, we may get a time out or grounded but as we grow the punishment can be as serious as expulsion from school or even going to jail. As we get older, the consequences for lying become greater.

Punishment never feels good.

Sometimes our parents can be very strict. They set rules for us to follow so that we can avoid being hurt or hurting others. These rules can feel restricting at times and we may break them every once in a while. If you break the rules, lying about it will not make things any better. Your parents may be disappointed in you if you do and will be forced to punish you.

If you tell the truth however, your punishment may be reduced. It is important to remember that even though you tell the truth, you still will be held accountable for your actions.

Kurious Kids Book about
Lying I ,Lying II and Sharing

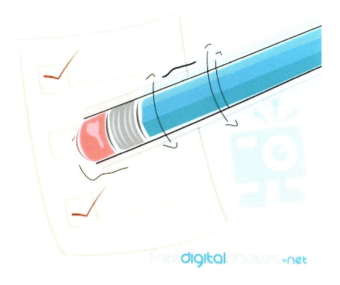

Lies cannot be erased, but they can be corrected.

You may think that getting a time out isn't as bad as it sounds, but consider that when you are facing a wall or sitting in a corner on your own, you may be missing out on a lot of fun. Being grounded is also not any fun. You may not be allowed to watch TV and therefore miss out on your favorite cartoons. Expulsion from school means that will be unable to receive an education and as a result life can be difficult when you are older if you cannot get a job and take care of yourself.

Lying pushes the things you love away.

Young adults and older people face even harsher punishments. Jail is a place that no one ever wants to go to. Having your freedom taken away can be devastating, thus it is important to avoid doing things that will allow this to happen.

Kurious Kids Book about
Lying I, Lying II and Sharing

Lying can separate you from the ones you love.

The best way to avoid these harsh consequences is to simply tell the truth.

What are the rewards for Honesty?

So what do you get for telling the truth?

The best gift you can give is the truth.

Aside from the respect, trust, love and admiration of others, sometimes there are physical rewards. A pat on the back is a lot nicer than a paddle on the butt! At school you can earn awards for hard work. If you play a sport, you can earn medals. When people recognize your efforts to be good and honest, they reward you in any way that they can.

Kurious Kids Book about
Lying I ,Lying II and Sharing

Honesty is very rewarding.

CONCLUSION

Remember, lying is always wrong. No matter what the circumstances are, the truth is the only way to bring resolve.

To help you remember why you should not lie, learn the song below written by Elsie Walner:

NEVER TELL A LIE

by Elsie Walner

Never tell a lie, even if in fun,

'Cause if you've told a lie,

Damage has been done.

Then nobody believes in you,

Whatever you may say,

Even if you speak the truth

And say it all the day.

So, always say what's real,

Always say what's true.

Oh, how good you'll feel

And we'll all believe in you.

We'll all believe in you.

Never tell a lie,

Nobody believes in you,

Whatever you may say,

Even if you speak the truth

And say it all the day.

So, always say what's real,

Always say what's true.

Oh, how good you'll feel

And we'll all believe in you.

We'll all believe

We'll all believe

We'll all believe in you.

We'll all believe

We'll all believe

We'll all believe in you.

The Kurious Kid Presents™:
Lying Part II

INTRODUCTION

What do you think about lying? Have you ever told a lie? What happened after you told it, and how did you feel? Is every kind of lie wrong? What about a lie that will keep someone's feelings from getting hurt? What is the real danger of lying in the first place? I mean, sure, it's good to be honest, but what damage can one teeny, tiny lie really do? Today, we are going to explore the answers to all of these questions and more!

Most lies start out small. When people begin to lie, they usually don't begin with a whopper of a made-up story. Instead, they tend to lie about things that seem little and harmless. For example, maybe your mom or dad has noticed cookies disappearing from the cookie jar and decides to ask you if you've eaten them. The truth is, you have, but you're afraid your parents might punish you or not let you have any more dessert if you say yes, so instead, you tell them you have no idea where all those cookies disappeared to.

What happens next? There are a couple different possibilities. First of all, your parents might be able to tell you're lying, and you'll end up being punished even worse than you would have been for just eating the cookies. Or, maybe they will believe you, and you'll get away with your lie, won't get punished, and will still be able to have dessert after dinner! This second possibility sounds great, doesn't it? You got away with your lie, and you're happy, your parents are happy—everybody wins! Or do they?

If you've ever told any sort of lie, you probably know that it isn't as simple as we've just made it sound. Sure, you might get away with something—but that doesn't mean you're going to be really and truly happy about it. Because what we didn't yet mention is the feeling of guilt that goes along with lying.

Guilt comes from your **conscience**, which is the part of your mind that tells you right from wrong. Everybody has a conscience. Your conscience is the reason that you know certain things are bad to do—hitting your little brother, stealing a candy bar from the grocery store check-out aisle, cheating on a test at school, making fun of someone in your class, throwing stones at animals, etc. Your conscience also tells you when things are right and gives you a good feeling about them—like when you help an older person across the street, or decide to rake your neighbor's front yard as well as your own, or pick up groceries for someone who dropped them.

But when it comes to lying, your conscience is programmed to give you a bad feeling—and that feeling is called *guilt*. What does guilt feel like? It's hard to explain. Some people say it makes them feel like their hearts are heavy, and they can't enjoy themselves until they decide to tell the truth or do the right thing. Other people feel very disappointed in themselves and can't stop thinking about what they did wrong. For some people, guilt is almost like a sort of pain that they can actually feel deep down inside. But whatever guilt feels like for you, there's one thing we can say for sure. Guilt *never* feels good!

It's good that we have guilt, though, because without guilt, it would be much simpler for us to do the wrong thing. Going back to the cookie jar example, imagine that you got away with your lie, and your parents didn't find out that you were the one who had actually eaten the cookies. You'd probably start to feel very guilty, and no matter what you did—play with a friend, watch your favorite TV show, eat a big bowl of ice cream—it wouldn't be nearly as much fun because the wrong thing you did would be bugging you. In fact, it just might bug you so much that you'd decide to go to your parents and tell them the truth. You might end up getting punished, but in the end, you'd feel a great weight off your shoulders because you had decided to do the right thing, after all!

Without the feeling of guilt, you see, it would be much easier to keep on lying about everything. *Why is lying such a bad thing in the first place?* you may be wondering. *I understand it's wrong, but* why? *What harm can one little fib actually do?* The answer to that is, a lot of harm! Let's take a look at some of the ways that lies can affect us and the people we love.

Lies Can Hurt People We Care About and Affect Our Relationships With Them.

That's right. Let's say one of your friends—we'll call her Lauren— asks you to come over to her house, but you don't feel like it. Instead of telling Lauren that another day might be better, you decide to tell her that your grandma is coming to visit, and you have to spend time with your family that day instead. Then another friend—we'll call him Mark—

comes along, and invites you over to play on the same day. You *do* feel like playing with him, so you tell him okay. After spending a while at Mark's house, the two of you decide to ride your bikes over to the park—and there on the swing set is Lauren! When she sees you playing with Mark, she realizes that you lied to her about your grandma coming over, and her feelings are very hurt.

A lie like that can cause your friends to think differently of you, to feel unappreciated and even disliked by you. How would *you* feel if you were Lauren? Even if you got an apology, it would take a little while before you could look at your friend the same way, wouldn't it?

Lies Can Affect How Other People Trust Us.

Let's imagine it's your grandma's birthday. Your grandpa is all excited about the gift he bought her, so he decides to let you in on the secret—he's getting her a kitten! You promise not to tell anyone, but that promise is a lie, because deep down inside, you're planning on telling your big sister. After all, you tell her everything. What harm can it do?

What you don't realize is that while you're telling your sister about the kitten, your big-mouth little brother is spying on you two. He's only four, and as soon as he hears about the new kitten, he gets so excited that he can't help but tell your grandma. Now the surprise is ruined, and it's all your fault! Your grandpa knows it had to have been you who told, because you're the only one who knew what the gift was. You feel terrible!

Then the holidays roll around, and your grandpa has another very special present to give your grandma. You can't wait for him to tell you what it is. You promise you won't share his secret with anyone else, and this time, you really mean it. But now it's too late, because your grandpa remembers how you lied about the birthday secret, and he doesn't trust you enough to risk sharing the holiday secret now. Can you really blame him for feeling that way? Wouldn't you?

Lies Can End Us Up in a Big-Time Mess.

There's an old saying that goes, "Oh, what a tangled web we weave, when first we practice to deceive." **Deceive** means the same thing as to lie, so basically what this expression means is that the more we lie, the bigger the mess we will find ourselves in. We'll get tangled up in our own lies, sort of like a fly gets tangled up in a spider web.

Imagine that you are having trouble concentrating in class because you're too busy whispering and passing notes back and forth with your best friend. Your teacher notices this, and gives you a warning, but somehow you and your friend keep on whispering. After her second warning, your teacher decides to send a note home to your parents, letting them know that you're not paying proper attention in school.

Suddenly you're very scared. You don't want your parents to be angry at you or disappointed in you, so you decide to get rid of the letter before you go home. You toss it in the garbage can in the school lobby (which is the exact same thing as lying because you're pretending that the letter never existed) before getting on the bus to go home. Both of your parents are still gone when you get there.

An hour later, your mom gets home, and a few minutes after that, your teacher happens to call to make sure she got the note. "Note? What note?" you hear your mom say. Immediately, you begin to panic. You don't have the note anymore, so how are you going to explain this to her?

Then you have your bright idea. Your mom wasn't here when the bus dropped you off, so you decide to say you walked home today and must have accidentally dropped the letter on your way. But you aren't counting on what happens next, because when your mom tells your teacher what you said, your teacher tells your mom that she *saw* you get on the bus this afternoon! Uh-oh!

You see, when you start telling lies and realizing that you're not going to get away with them, you'll just try to come up with more lies to cover for yourself—until, before you know it, you've landed yourself in a whopper of a mess! Now you're in trouble for not only talking in class, but also for throwing away the letter, and for lying about walking home on top of it!

As you can see, lies—even lies that seem small and unimportant—can only end us and our loved ones up in pain, sadness, heartache, distrust, punishment, and more! Is anything ever worth making a friend or family member feel bad about themselves, or feel differently about you? Is anything ever worth losing the trust of someone you love and care about? Is anything ever worth winding yourself up in a big mess over something that started out small, like a letter? The answer is no!

No matter how tempted you may feel to lie, or how easily you think you could get yourself out of trouble just by twisting the truth, stop for a moment to think about what you've learned. No lie is ever *really* harmless. If you respect yourself and the other people in your life, you will decide to do the right thing by telling the truth in every situation.

But wait! you may be saying. *What about those times when you sort of* have *to lie to keep from hurting someone's feelings?* Okay. Let's think about that. We'll just say your favorite aunt got a brand-new haircut, and she's all excited to show you. But when she steps through the door, smiling a mile wide, you're horrified—her hair is a mess; it looks like someone cut it with a butcher knife in their sleep!

Kurious Kids Book about
Lying I, Lying II and Sharing

"How do you like my hair?" your aunt asks, striking a pose. What are you supposed to do? If you say you love it, that would be a lie. But if you tell your aunt the truth—that you hate her haircut—that would really make her feel bad. In a situation like this, you don't have to come right out and tell her, "I hate your hair!" because that *would* be hurtful. But you also shouldn't lie. After all, your aunt may really be looking for your advice—should she keep getting her hair cut like this, or let it grow back to its old style?

Try a creative answer that involves telling the truth *kindly*, such as, "Oh, Aunt Maureen, you're always beautiful, but actually I think I liked your old hair style better." That way, you can make her feel good by giving her a compliment, but at the same time, you're *not* lying! Who knows? Aunt Maureen just might listen up and never make that same *hair*-brained mistake again!

So, is it ever okay to lie? The answer is no! Another old expression tells us that "Honesty is the best policy." Basically, this means that when you're honest, you can know for sure that you're on the right track. Even when it's hard to be honest, it sure beats all the awful things that could happen because of a lie!

And *that's* the truth!

The Kurious Kid Presents™:

Sharing

THINK ABOUT SHARING

Have you ever thought about sharing? Do you like to share your things? Do you think that sharing is important? The truth is that sharing is **very** important. If you don't think so, then think about this. Has this ever happened to you? When your friends come over to play at your house, you bring out some of your toys so that everyone can have fun and play with them. But sometimes when you go over to one of your friend's homes to play, they won't share their toys with you!

Now how does that make you feel? Do you think it is fair that you share your toys, but your friend does not share their toys with you? Do you have a friend that always has to go first? Wouldn't you like to have a chance to go first sometimes too? These are all a part of sharing whether you are sharing your toys, or sharing who goes first.

When do you have the most fun playing? Is it when everyone is taking their turn, following the rules and having fun? Well, that is usually when everyone has the most fun. So what about your friend that doesn't like to share? Did you know that **you** could help them to share too? Surprised? Then read on.

Kurious Kids Book about
Lying I ,Lying II and Sharing

Girls having fun playing together and sharing toys

Helping Others To Share

Anyone that has a younger brother or sister knows that sharing isn't always an easy thing to do. If your brother or sister is 2 ½ years old or younger, then the word you probably hear the most is, "**MINE!**" Then they may grab the toy away. The first thing you need to understand is that at that age they are too young to know how to share.

But you can still help them to learn how to share. Younger children learn by watching. You can help by setting an example. This can be as easy as the next time you are eating a cookie, and your little brother or sister wants a cookie too, then break off a small piece and share it with them. Or take out a toy that you know they will like to play with. Starting playing with it, and chances are they will come over and want to play too. If it is a toy like building blocks, you can start sharing by handing your brother or sister one block at a time to help them start to build something. They may end up taking the box of blocks away and playing by themselves, but in that small time that you spent together, they were learning about sharing and spending fun time with you.

Here are some toys that a younger brother or sister may like to play with

My Friend Won't Share Their Toys!

We have talked about helping a younger brother or sister start to learn how to share. But what can you do about a friend that refuses to share their toys? You may feel bad that when your friend comes over to your house, you share your toys with them, but when you go over to their house they just will not let you play with their toys. After all, what is fair is fair! Besides, they have some great toys that you would really enjoy playing with!

So what can you do? The answer can be easier than you think. If there is one special toy that they will not let you play with, you can tell them that you understand that that toy may be one that is extra special, and they may not want to share that one. But what toys do they have that they are willing to share so that everyone can play and have fun?

If they aren't sure what toys they may have, you may be able to make some suggestions like coloring, or playing with cars or trains. Sometimes you can both play with different toys, and still be playing together. The important thing is being able to play together and have fun.

Kurious Kids Book about
Lying I, Lying II and Sharing

You can make suggestions to your friends on what toys you enjoy playing with

Sometimes Sharing Means Compromise

Uh Oh! You really did it this time! You wanted to play with one of your favorite board games, but you and your brother or sister just could not agree on who will go first. You wanted to the red pieces but they did too. You get to feeling that this is just not fair! Your brother or sister got to use the red pieces the last two times you played the game. You wanted to be that color this time!

So what did you do? You started to argue with your brother or sister, and this made Mom mad. What is the result? Now no one can play with the game! Mom has taken it away until you can both get along and agree on how to play.

What can you do now? One answer is to compromise! The game sitting up high on a shelf with no one playing with it isn't doing anyone any good. Right now does it matter who goes first, and who uses the red pieces? The answer in one word is no.

At times like this, a compromise may be an answer. Talk to your brother or sister, and work out the problem. Tell them that they can go first if you can use the red pieces. Or let them use the red pieces this time, and you can use the red pieces the next time you play. If that still doesn't work, then suggest that no one use the red pieces this time, and that both of you have to pick different color pieces. Who knows? You might even wind up laughing when you see just how silly you were to fight over it in the first place!

Arguing isn't the answer. Sharing sometimes means making a compromise.

Sometimes You Have To Share People Too

You have been **so** excited ever since you heard the news that your grandfather will be coming for a visit! He always tells the best stories. You were hoping to be able to spend some time alone together on this visit, just you and him. But unfortunately, your grandfather will only be able to spend just a few days on his visit this time, so it does not look like you will be able to spend that special time alone together.

You still want to enjoy every minute you can while he is visiting. So you start thinking what can you do? Then the idea comes to you! You just got a great book out of the library. It would be the **perfect** book for your grandfather to read to you, and he can read it to your brothers or sisters too! It would be something that everyone can gather around and enjoy. Cuddling up close to your grandfather and hearing him read is a very special treat indeed.

Sharing family time can be very special, and something that everyone in the family can enjoy together.

People Aren't The Only Ones That Share

Sharing is important, and it is one reason that many people and animals can get along so well. Are you surprised that animals share too? One place where you can see this harmony among animals is at a birdfeeder.

A birdfeeder is an interesting thing to watch. When the birdfeeder is full of seeds, and the birds know they can come to the feeder, and eat in safety, the show begins! Often times, many of the same types will come and eat at the birdfeeder together. Usually, the smaller birds come first to feed such as the sparrows. Many of the sparrows gather around the feeder together from all different sides, eating up the seeds that were placed there for them to enjoy.

After a while, you may notice that these smaller birds will leave the feeder so that the next group of larger birds can come to feed next. The next group of birds gathers close to the feeder, and sits waiting on nearby branches for their turn to eat at the feeder. This cycle goes on for quite a few times, until all the birds from smallest to the largest, get a chance to eat at the feeder. In the picture below, the large horse is sharing its food and bucket with the pigeons. Other pigeons are lined up on the sidewalk waiting for their turn to feed.

An example of how animals can share with each other.

Sharing Can Be Fun!

There are so many things you can say about sharing, but another very important thing to remember is that sharing can also be fun! Is there something that you can remember that you did together as group that you had fun doing? Here is one activity that many people can do together. It is something that everyone from the youngest to the oldest family member can enjoy doing.

Baking! Especially those wonderful hand decorated cookies! Think about all the teamwork and sharing that is involved. A parent needs to be in charge of doing anything with the oven, and making sure how much of each ingredient gets put into the batter. But there are still plenty of things that everyone else can do!

One person can read out the ingredients that will be needed for the recipe. Someone else can gather up those ingredients and place them on the table so that they are ready to use. But there are still more jobs to go around! One person under an adult's supervision can measure up all the ingredients and put them in the mixing bowl, while someone else stirs all the ingredients together. If these are the kind of cookies that can be decorated, then everyone can decorate some cookies however they would like to, and use whatever colors they wish. Let your creativity soar!

What teamwork! What fun! Let's not forget about the most delicious part of all – eating some of those special cookies warm from the oven! Yum!

Baking can be a fun, sharing project that everyone can do together. Here the youngest member of the family is waiting her turn to decorate the cookies, and is coloring in the meantime.

There Are Many Things You Can Share

We have talked about sharing many different things. These have been mostly physical things. Physical things are things that you can see, feel or touch, like toys or food. But did you know that you could share things that are invisible too? Can you name some examples of what might be invisible things you can share?

Some invisible things that you can share are your feelings, thoughts, or ideas. You can share in a conversation with someone when you talk with them. These are all things you can share, yet you cannot physically see them, they are invisible.

There are many places in your home where you share both physical and invisible types of sharing each and every day. There is one place where the whole family gathers and does this each day. Can you think of where that might be? You are right if you guessed at the family table.

The family table is a very special place. Perhaps you share in some of the chores that need to get done, and one of those chores is to set the table. Each time you sit down to the table, you and your wonderful family are sharing in food to eat and conversation. When someone may ask you, "What did you do in school today?" You are sharing what has happened to you. You are sharing your day, maybe some thoughts and ideas you have, and by doing this, you are sharing in conversation. All of that is happening at your table every day. Now you can see why it is such a special place!

Kurious Kids Book about
Lying I ,Lying II and Sharing

Many things are shared at the family table, such as feelings, ideas and conversation

Are You Already Sharing?

Sharing is an interesting idea. One way you may define sharing is when you consider others before you think about yourself. This could mean that you may take something that you already have, and share it with others. You might share anything from food such as a cookie, to a game that many people can play and enjoy.

Another way to share is when you share your time. Have you ever helped someone in your class? Maybe you helped them by sharing something you know how to do. You might have helped them with a hard word in reading, or helped them solve a math problem. Perhaps you are good at sports, and you were sharing with them the best way to kick, catch or throw a ball. Whether you share your time, or share your knowledge, both are good examples of sharing. So you see? You may already be sharing, and you didn't even know it!

You can share many things with others such as your knowledge

Sometimes I Do Not Like To Share

There may be something that you have that is really special to you, and because it is so very special, you would rather not share it with anyone else. If that is true, then don't feel bad, because you are not alone. Many people have something that they cherish above everything else. This special something could be anything like a plush toy, a piece of jewelry, a music box, a model plane or train, or it could be a doll. There could be many reasons why this item is so special to you. One reason could be that you have had it for a long time, and it has many memories for you. Or your special item was a project that you worked on for a long time, and you think it could get broken if someone else played with it and wasn't very careful.

As you can see, there are many reasons why something can be very important to you. There is nothing wrong with not wanting to share this special thing with others. Here are a few things you may want to keep in mind. When you have friends over, don't take out this special toy. If a friend reaches for your special item, you could say, "I'm sorry, please don't play with that. Let's find something else to play with." Then you should try and find a game or something that you can both play with and enjoy.

Unfortunately, not all of your friends are going to be as gentle as you are with your favorite things. It is important that your friends respect your wishes not to play with something. You also need to respect your friends' wishes if they have something that they do not want you to play with. You do not always have to share everything.

Sometimes you may have something that you do not want to share with others

Sharing In Sports

When you stop to think about it, sharing is everywhere around you. There is even sharing when it comes to sports. A team can, "Share in the win." Whenever a team wins, then every member of the team is a winner too! There is no one player that can make up the whole team. A team is a group of people all working together, and challenging themselves to play and do their best.

You can pick any sport where there is more than one player. Football, baseball, soccer, basketball, ice hockey or rowing, it is still the same each time. In order to win, each player relies on another member of the team and together, they work towards winning.

Let's pick baseball for an example. Once the pitcher pitches the ball, and the batter hits the ball, the pitcher is not going to leave the mound and run all the way to the outfield to try and catch it. Instead, the pitcher will rely on one of the outfielders to catch the ball, or to chase the ball down. The outfielder may need to scoop up the ball, and will then rely on the first base team player to catch the ball that is thrown. As you can see, each player relies on another player, and together they make a team. This is a great example of sharing.

Teamwork and sharing is an important part in sports

Sharing is a Form of Caring

There are many ways to show that you care. One way of showing that you care is when you share. You may share your toys with your friends to show that you care about them as your friends. You may share a hug with someone in your family to show your love.

Sometimes things may happen and you just don't know what you can do to help. You want to help, but you just don't know how. This might make you may feel helpless. Perhaps you feel like you are only one person, so what can you do? The answer is plenty!

Never forget that sharing means that other people are involved too. Perhaps something has happened and you would like to help by sending a donation like supplies or money. Stop and think for a moment. If you feel this way, maybe others feel this way too. Maybe they would like to help, but don't know how. If this is true, now you have more than one person that would like to get involved. It may be a community project, or a school or church project. There are many ways to share in a project, and we will talk more about that next.

You can make a difference when you share

Share in a Project

There could be many ways that you could take part in a project. One project could be a community project. Many communities take pride in where they live and want to beautify it anyway they can. This could involve picking up litter in the area, or cleaning out a vacant lot. Many communities have come together and built a community playground for all to enjoy. Or others have gotten together and painted beautiful paintings on what used to be an eye sore. Still other communities have gotten together and started to plant gardens with flowers, or vegetable gardens. You can speak with an adult to find out what community activities are happening in your area and then get involved.

Another way to share in a project could be to raise funds or supplies to help with an event that may have happened. You can speak with an adult or a teacher to see if your school could help out. There are many ways you can help. Perhaps your school could hold a bake sale, or a book sale to raise funds for the event. Maybe in your school, you wear uniforms. Your school could hold a uniform free day. On this day, you do not have to wear your uniform to school, if you donate money or supplies to the cause. So, as you can see, there are many ways you can share, and there are many things you and others can do to help and make a difference!

Example of a Community Project: A Community Garden

Something to Try: Share in a Family Project

We have talked about sharing in large projects like a community or a school project. But there are other projects you can get involved with too. How about working together as a family and sharing in a family project? Sounds like fun? Well it certainly can be!

Talk to an adult about something that the whole family can do together. Think of ideas that everyone can work on and share doing together. Just think how nice it will be when your project is done, and you know that you have all had fun working on it together.

Think if there is a project or something you have all wanted and make it or build it together. Some possible projects may be to build a birdhouse or bird feeder together. You can all go together to buy the things you will need to build it. The nails, wood and paint. An adult will need to cut the pieces out and perhaps put the pieces together, but everyone can help with painting or decorating the birdhouse. Just think how happy you will be when the first bird comes to feed from the feeder, or lives in the house that you all built together!

Another possible project could be to make a gingerbread house. You can make one from scratch. Everyone could have a chance to work together to make the batter, and then everyone could have fun decorating it. There are many projects you can consider doing together as a family project.

Family Project: A Gingerbread House

Share a Day; Share a Memory

As we have discussed earlier, sharing can also be something invisible too. You can share a day with someone, and when you do, you can share a memory you can always remember. It doesn't have to be anything fancy, just something that is special to you, and that you enjoy doing.

Think about the things you enjoy doing, and then you can suggest to an adult or friend putting a day aside when you can do your favorite thing. Maybe you enjoy camping. Perhaps one weekend, your family can get together and enjoy camping in the great outdoors. Can't get away? No problem! Maybe you can pitch a tent in your own backyard. If it is too cold to go outside, then it is still not a problem! A few blankets draped across a table can make for an excellent inside tent. It is the perfect place for sleeping, or gathering together to tell stories.

Whatever it is that you enjoy the most, anything from fishing to a day at the park, what is important is that you enjoy your special day, and when you do, you will also find out that doing the activity is only half the fun. One the best parts is **sharing** your special day with someone, and enjoying all the fun you had!

Sharing a special day and creating memories

Share Your Feelings

Feelings can be such odd things sometimes. There are times when you are so happy that you want to share those feelings with everyone. You want everyone to know what has happened, to make you feel so great.

These are very good feelings, and you would like everyone to feel happy and to share in your happiness.

But what about the times when you may not feel so happy, in fact, you may even feel a bit sad. Did you ever notice that you are not as quick to share those unhappy feelings? Many things can make you feel sad. It could be something that happened at school, or having a fight with your best friend. You may think that everyone knows what is going on, and that they should know exactly how you feel. But the simple truth is how can they know? Were they there with you when you had a bad day at a school? Were they with you when you had a fight with your best friend over something that was no doubt silly? Unless they were there, the answer is that they will not know what has happened. It is up to you to share your feelings.

When you talk things over with a trusted adult, you can feel better just by talking about whatever is on your mind and bothering you. By talking things over, you can many times come up with answers to your problem. But when you don't talk about it, no one can ever help you because you have never shared what is wrong! Now you can see how important it is to share your feelings whether they are happy or sad.

Sharing your feelings is important

Share Your Dreams

Dreams can be very interesting and something that is unique just to you! Dreams can be funny or sad, silly or serious. Sometimes things that you see on television, or in the movies can have a way of reappearing in your dreams. Many times you may play a leading role in your dreams. You could be the hero that comes to the rescue, or have some kind of super power that helps you to combat bad or evil. Other times, you may be a super athlete that comes through and scores the win for the team. Maybe you are a super sleuth and you solve mysteries when you are asleep. Your dreams may be so silly at times that they just don't make any sense, and you can't help but to laugh at how very silly they are. Nightmares or scary dreams can happen to anyone from time to time. But if you have too many nightmares, or the same nightmare, then it is time to speak to an adult about it.

When you fall asleep isn't the only time when you dream. There are other dreams that you may have. One day, you may have decided that you want to be a doctor, nurse, therapist, skilled athlete, actor or actress or whatever your heart desires. You can also share these dreams and wishes with an adult or your teacher. They can have good ways on how you can reach your dreams. Dreams whether you are awake or asleep are a part of you, and something you can share with others.

An example of what you may dream about

Share Your Thoughts and Ideas

If you are a part of any group or club, there may be times when you are asked to share your thoughts and ideas on something. This can be anything from asking for suggestions on how to do something, or asking for help in planning an event. The questions may be easy like, "What color balloons should we use to decorate with?" Or harder questions like, "Our school needs new band uniforms, what can we do to help raise money?" You may also be asked to share your ideas on how to improve something. You may need to give your ideas on how to make your school seem friendlier to new students.

One thing to remember is that you are an individual. No one thinks exactly the same way as you do, and you do not think exactly the same way as they do. That is one reason that things are always so interesting and exciting! When a group of people gets together to improve or discuss things, all different kinds of thoughts and ideas are shared. You may have an idea that no one else thought of, and someone else can have a suggestion that you would never have thought about. Sharing your thoughts, ideas and suggestions can go a long way in making things better. People may not always agree with your ideas, but they should respect your thoughts, as well as you respecting their point of view.

There are many ways to share your thoughts and ideas

Sharing: How To Get Started

After reading about sharing, you may be thinking that sharing sounds like something you may be interested in doing more of. If so, then the first question you may be asking yourself is, "What is the best way to get started?" Well, the first thing to ask yourself is, "What is it you would most like to do?" Are you interested in starting on a family project? Maybe working on a community project, or a school project sounds like something you would be interested in trying.

If you are interested in starting to work on a family project, talk to someone in your family. Tell them what you would like to do, and see what suggestions they may have. If joining in a community project is something you would like to try, speak to an adult. They can help you get involved with the people running the project. If a school project has your interest, then speaking with a teacher is a great place to start. If you have a friend that is already involved in working on projects, ask them what projects they are working on, and ask if you can join too.

You may want to work more on being able to express yourself better. Speak with a parent, and tell them what you are trying to do. They may be able to give you some great suggestions. As you already know, there are many ways to share. Now you just have to find the one you are the most interested in doing.

Getting started on the road to sharing is easier than you may think

Sharing: A Summary

Hopefully after reading about sharing you have learned some new and interesting things, and perhaps now look at sharing and the many ways to share in a different way. One of the best things about sharing is that it is never too soon, or ever too late to start to share. From the very first gooey cookie a toddle may offer to share with you, all the way to being involved in a project, they are all a part of sharing.

As we talked about, sharing can be done in many ways. If you feel that you are selfish with your toys and you don't want to share **any** of them, then you can speak with a parent and let them know that you would like to work on your sharing skills. Share with them the fact that you do not want to share any of your toys, even when your friends share their toys with you. Sharing is something that should be fun, and as you begin to share, you should see that you enjoy sharing and that it makes you feel good.

There are so very many ways to share. If you already share your thoughts and feelings, hopefully you will continue doing it. If you have a hard time telling others how you feel, then now is a good time to let a parent know. Just keep in mind that everyone is different, and what one person may like to do may not be what you enjoy doing. That is fine because everyone is different. What is important is to respect everyone for their own feelings and ideas, the same way that you would like them to respect you. Have you learned anything new about sharing?

Kurious Kids Book about
Lying I ,Lying II and Sharing

Check Out My Other Books

Below you'll find some of my other popular books that are popular on Amazon and Kindle as well. Simply click on the links below to check them out.

http://www.amazon.com/How-Start-Successful-Hair-Salon-ebook/dp/B00ED8F7EO

http://www.amazon.com/Opening-Boutique-Guide-Clothing-Starting-ebook/dp/B00EOAVAN8

http://www.amazon.com/Becoming-coupon-Warrior-Extreme-couponing-ebook/dp/B00LO8KCBY

http://www.amazon.com/Online-Marketing-Real-Estate-Professionals-ebook/dp/B00EF5DTH2

http://www.amazon.com/How-Read-Body-Language-101-ebook/dp/B00HBUA35E

http://www.amazon.com/Clothing-Line-Start-Guide-Successful-ebook/dp/B00EEWE0PQ

http://www.amazon.com/How-Start-Rap-Record-Label-ebook/dp/B00EE6RAOA

http://www.amazon.com/Hip-Hop-Rhyming-Dictionary-Extensive-ebook/dp/B00FF8SDZ6

http://www.amazon.com/Start-Restaurant-Without-Losing-Shirt-ebook/dp/B00EETB6Y2

http://www.amazon.com/Play-Piano-Fast-Yourself-Playing-ebook/dp/B00LUQ1SKO

http://www.amazon.com/Fashion-Show-Secrets-guide-fashion-ebook/dp/B00LUPNPTW

Kurious Kids Book about
Lying I ,Lying II and Sharing

Thank You for Your Purchase!!!!!

Thank you again for Ordering this book!

I hope this book was able to provide you with the Information that you were searching for. Lastly, if you REALLY enjoyed this book, then I'd like to ask you for a favor, would you be kind enough to leave a review for this book on Amazon? It'd be greatly appreciated!

Lastly, Please be sure to connect with us We Would Love to Hear from You

Bull City Publishing Social Media Links:

Blog: http://bullcitypublishing.com/blog/

Facebook Group:
https://www.facebook.com/groups/bullcitypublishing/

Twitter : https://twitter.com/BullCityPub

Instagram: http://instagram.com/bullcitypublishing

Pintrest: https://pintrest.com/bullcitypub

Linkedin: http://www.linkedin.com/companies/5311112

Tumblr: http://bullcitypublishing.tumblr.com

Do you Love Reading? Do you Want a Ton of FREE Kindle Books? Join our Mailing list by Emailing us at freebooks@bullcitypublishing.com

Do you Need Help Writing a Book? Would you like to get published? If So Shoot us an email publish@bullcitypublishing.com

Thank you and good luck!

James Moore

Printed in Poland
by Amazon Fulfillment
Poland Sp. z o.o., Wrocław